THE POTTY WARS

UNDERSTANDING AND HELPING YOUR ENCOPRETIC CHILD

LIBBY ROBBINS, PH.D.

CONTENTS

INTRODUCTION

When I began my private practice, my first patient was a five-year-old girl who suffered from chronic constipation and soiling. In every other way, she was a bright, good-natured little girl, but her toileting behavior was driving her parents crazy. Her mother was worried, embarrassed, and defensive, after years of listening to well-intentioned, but ineffective advice from her mother, other relatives, and friends. Her father was certain that his daughter was acting willfully, and that if she were punished enough, she would "snap out of it." There were regular angry exchanges between parents and child over using the toilet, and frequent disagreements between the parents about how to handle the situation.

In my first meeting with the parents, I was rather baffled about the cause of this symptom, which was clearly uncomfortable for the child, and unpleasant for the whole family. Yet, a dim prickling at the edge of my memory made me think I had encountered this problem before. Upon reflection, I recalled a boy, named "Joey" in my class of three and four-year-olds at the daycare center where I taught after receiving my Masters degree in Special Education. Joey soiled himself several times a week, and it was my job to clean and change him. I remembered how frustrated and angry I got over having to do this unpleasant chore, when all he had to do was tell me he needed to use the toilet. After I left the daycare center for a job in Special Education, I discussed Joey with my supervisor, who was a child psychiatrist. She informed me that he was probably suffering from a disorder called encopresis, and that he needed therapy rather than discipline.

Fortunately, my first case responded well to play therapy and parent guidance work. During my work with the little girl, it became clear that withholding stool was a symptom of her powerful anxiety about the safety of her body and her ability to contain her angry impulses. Exploring those issues with her, and helping her parents to disengage from the battle for control they were waging against their daughter were key factors in resolving the problem.

No sooner had I finished congratulating myself for managing to stumble my way to a satisfactory resolution, than another set of parents with another encopretic child appeared in my office. Before I knew it, I had been discovered by the Pediatric Gastroenterology community, and a steady stream of young children with encopresis was parading through my office. I was stunned by the number of families who were struggling with this disorder; but when I tried to find information about the mental health aspects of encopresis, there was little available. There were plenty of articles about medical and behavioral treatments for encopresis, but only a handful of publications in the mental health journals, and even fewer resources for parents, who were hungry for information and advice about their children.

Over the years, I have worked with over one hundred encopretic children and their families. Parents regularly ask me for the name of a book they can read to learn about toileting problems, and are frustrated when I have little to offer. I used to joke that there is no book to read because I haven't written it yet. Parents were not amused. One mother even offered to help me write the book. So, with endless gratitude to all the children and parents who have taught me about encopresis over the years, I have conquered my writers' "constipation" and produced this book. I hope it provides you with information about your child, and some useful techniques to try at home. You may decide to consult a mental health professional about your encopretic child. Whatever your situation may be, I hope this book will be helpful to you, even if just to reassure you that you are in good company with other parents who are trying their best to help their children with a difficult problem.

Before I begin, it's important for me to let you know that the vignettes of parents and children in these pages are created from composites of families I have worked with. None of the names or descriptions represent actual people or their circumstances.

A final warning: I occasionally attempt to use humor in this book. Encopresis is a serious, upsetting condition, and I do not take it lightly. On the other hand, I don't want to write or subject you to a dry professional thesis. Let's face it, this is a book about pooping and children - two topics that are both professionally interesting and endlessly amusing to me.

PART I

UNDERSTANDING ENCOPRESIS

CHAPTER 1

WHAT IS ENCOPRESIS ANYWAY?

Sam's mother, Linda, is beginning to feel frantic. Sam is supposed to be in a pre-kindergarten class five days a week at his preschool this fall. The school has made it clear that Sam cannot attend the program unless he is potty trained. By the end of last year, his teacher was pretty fed-up with Sam's daily accidents, and complained to Linda on several occasions. She advised Linda to let Sam spend a weekend in the house without wearing any diaper or underwear, certain that he would be forced to use the potty when the urge struck. Linda forced a smile and thanked her for the suggestion, but sighed to herself. She had tried the bare bottom method months ago, to the detriment of her family room carpeting. In fact, Linda was pretty sure she had tried every trick in the book to train Sam, with no success. He simply refused to use the potty – even the one that played music – and only pooped in a pull-up after holding in his stool for days at a time. Linda felt that she could live with the pull-ups if it weren't for the continual small accidents several times a day. The mess and odor were so embarrassing for Linda (although apparently not for Sam) that she was uncomfortable taking him to playdates, restaurants, or even his grandparents' house. They really didn't go anywhere that Linda could not swiftly and discreetly launch a clean-up operation when Sam soiled himself. It seemed to Linda that her world revolved around Sam's bowel movements, and she was becoming increasingly angry at her own helplessness and Sam's stubbornness. Linda doesn't know it yet, but she is dealing with an encopretic child.

The Diagnostic and Statistical Manual (DSM-IV-TR, 2000) is the reference used by mental health professionals, which lists all of the possible mental health diagnoses, along with their symptoms. Encopresis is defined by the DSM-IV-TR as the passage of stool in inappropriate places at least once a month for three months by children ages four and older, for which no physical cause can be found. There are two types of encopresis: encopresis with constipation and overflow incontinence; and encopresis without constipation and overflow incontinence. In addition, encopresis may be primary, when the child has never successfully toilet trained, and secondary, when the child was toilet trained for a period of time and then began having accidents.

Estimates are that between 1.5% and 7% of children suffer from encopresis, with a higher incidence in boys than in girls. Between 85% and 90% of encopresis cases are the type associated with constipation and overflow incontinence. Children with this type of encopresis often withhold their bowel movements until they become constipated. When there is a solid mass of stool held in the child's colon, liquid stool seeps around the mass and out of the anus, causing soiling. While this is the most common type of encopresis, there are other reasons children poop in their pants past the age at which most children are potty trained. I will talk more about these issues later.

Before proceeding, I want to be clear that, in my experience, encopresis is not usually associated with serious cognitive or emotional disabilities; however some children with serious problems have encopresis as well. Some of the signs that your child needs to have a comprehensive psychiatric evaluation include:

1. Other developmental delays.
2. Deliberate pooping outside of underpants or a diaper in inappropriate places, such as the living room carpet or the middle of your bed.
3. Smearing or playing with feces after the age of two.
4. Bizarre, graphically violent, or inappropriately sexual thoughts.
5. Impulsive or aggressive behavior that threatens the safety of self or others.
6. Sadness, tearfulness, or inability to enjoy life that lasts for more than two weeks.

These are possible signs of more serious conditions that require immediate attention.

For most parents, their encopretic children seem to be developing relatively normally except for this one, stubborn and unpleasant problem...

CHAPTER 2

A DEVELOPMENTAL PERSPECTIVE ON ENCOPRESIS

As she happily anticipated the birth of her first child, Carla thought carefully about what kind of mother she would be, and what her daughter would be like. Carla's mother had not been particularly nurturing or empathic, and Carla remembered being a timid, worried child who rarely succeeded in winning her mother's approval despite her best efforts. She was determined to be warm, loving, and supportive with her children. She imagined happy outings with the jogging stroller, chatting with friends at Starbucks while the baby slept in her sling, and quiet afternoons at home playing, looking at books together, and singing to the baby when she was fussy. Carla certainly never imagined *this*. Lenore was diagnosed with severe reflux shortly after birth, when she began projectile vomiting. Zantac seemed to help Lenore keep her feedings down, but she remained colicky and difficult to soothe. Carla's dates for coffee usually had to be canceled because Lenore was screaming inconsolably, and her quiet afternoons of bonding with her child dissolved in tears – Lenore's and Carla's. Carla's husband, Rich, wanted to be helpful; but he worked long hours so that Carla could afford to stay home with Lenore. By the time he came home, Lenore was usually in bed, Carla was exhausted and depleted, and Rich was at a loss as to how to be supportive. His well-intentioned advice made Carla furious, so eventually Rich began retreating to his computer in the evenings to avoid Carla.

Just when Lenore seemed to be feeling better and Carla was getting her feet under her, it was time for potty training. Lenore flatly refused to be in the same room with the potty. She continued to urinate in her diaper and hid behind the sofa when she needed to have a bowel movement. Changing her diaper was a nightmare, because Lenore thrashed and screamed like a banshee. Carla worried that a neighbor might hear the racket and report her for abusing Lenore. Even worse, Carla worried that she might snap and abuse Lenore. Carla's mother was free with her criticism of Carla's mothering. She accused Carla of spoiling Lenore and admonished her to toughen up. The pediatrician advised Carla to relax, stop pressuring Lenore to use the potty, and let her train when she was ready. Nothing seemed to help – Carla tried toughening up, relaxing, rewarding, punishing, ignoring, reasoning, pleading – but, if anything, the situation appeared to be getting worse.

Now Lenore was nearly five years old, and although she sometimes peed in the toilet, she still had daily urine accidents. Lenore never pooped in the potty, and Carla discovered that Lenore was going behind the sofa to hide while she struggled to hold in her stool. The stool softener prescribed by the pediatrician made it harder for Lenore to hold her poop, so she began letting out small amounts into her pull-up several times a day instead of having a normal bowel movement.

In addition, the small injuries of childhood sent Lenore into hysterics, she would not sit still to get her hair cut, and a visit to the dentist resulted in such an embarrassing tantrum that Carla never took her back. At the suggestion of her pediatrician, Carla took Lenore to the gastroenterologist to see if she had a gastrointestinal disorder that was the cause of her toileting problems. After a regimen of laxatives, stool softeners, and a behavior plan failed to produce results, the gastroenterologist referred Carla to a child therapist to address the psychological causes of Lenore's encopresis. Carla and Rich didn't know whether to be horrified or relieved.

Some parents are surprised when physicians refer them to a child therapist because medical interventions failed to treat their children's encopresis. Other parents have suspected all along that their children were holding in their stools for psychological and emotional reasons. In fact, most clinicians believe that encopresis is caused by a combination of physical and emotional factors. Research studies have looked at the specific causes of encopresis, with limited success. The only strong link which has been established is between encopresis and constipation; however, the studies disagree about whether constipation causes encopresis, or encopresis causes constipation. There is some evidence linking encopresis to anxiety, ADHD, behavior problems, and stress. None of the research has found clear causes for encopresis. Part of the reason for the lack of clarity is that encopresis is most likely influenced by multiple factors in the life of a child.

During the time I have been providing mental health treatment to children with encopresis, I have noticed developmental and psychological themes that recur frequently in encopretic children. Before going into a detailed description of the psychology of encopresis, it is helpful to look at the developmental tasks facing the young child around the time potty training begins. These are challenges that all children face at around two to four years of age. Understanding what young children are trying to accomplish is necessary in order to see where development has gone off track.

The Preschool Years: Not All Fun and Games

Somewhere between the second and third year of life, most children begin to develop control over their bladder and bowel functions.

As the child becomes aware of this new ability to decide when to hold and when to release his body's products, he becomes quite interested in his bodily functions. Pee and poop, and the places where they emerge become a focus for the child's curiosity.

As children begin to take special note of their bodies, they cannot help but notice differences between girls and boys. Some children become aware of the difference between the sexes even earlier, at around eighteen months, and may exhibit some curiosity, but rarely seem worried by their discovery. By the time the child is two or three, it is a different story. Suddenly the difference between boys and girls becomes a subject of concern. To a small child, it appears that boys have a body part that is missing on girls. Where did it go? Suddenly, previously carefree toddlers develop fears about injuries to their bodies. While this is certainly an uncomfortable stage for the young child, most eventually come to the understanding that girls are made differently, and have their own special equipment which is mostly on the inside. Until this realization dawns, parents may notice that their child is panicked by minor booboos, and feel as if they are singlehandedly keeping the bandaid industry afloat. Some children also become fearful of having their hair or nails cut, or even worry that part of them might get sucked down the bathtub drain. The life of a three-year-old child is far from carefree!

Just at this already stressful time for the child, toilet training is usually introduced. Suddenly the young child finds that he has been endowed with the superpower to delight or frustrate his parents simply by depositing his pee and poop in or out of the potty. Now he must decide whether to use his new powers for good or evil!

Although most children are motivated to please their parents, this choice is not as clear cut for the child as it is for the parents. At the same time as the child is learning to exercise greater control over his body, he is also feeling a strong desire to break free of parental control and establish his independence. Power struggles with Mom and Dad are the order of the day. What better arena could there be for exerting ones will than in the bathroom? Now there's a battle that parents simply can't win!

In most cases, after some minor skirmishes, the child decides that using the toilet pleases him as much as it pleases his parents, and he permits toilet training to succeed. Parents may congratulate themselves on a job well done, but without the child's cooperation, the potty remains empty. Parents of encopretic children know this all too well.

To further complicate matters, just as the young child is feeling a powerful developmental push towards independence, he is also becoming more aware of the world outside his immediate family. He is often attending pre-school or daycare, forming relationships with teachers, childcare providers, and peers, and spending more and more time away from home. At this point, many children realize that they have a problem: they wish to be free from parental domination, but they need their parents to protect them from the dangers in the outside world. This conflict can create a great deal of internal turmoil, as the child struggles to reconcile these competing desires.

This is the age when shouts of "I can do it myself" alternate with wails of "I can't do it!" Children who were fearless adventurers a few months before suddenly slam on the brakes and peer cautiously from behind Mother's or Father's leg. Parents may find this a perplexing and frustrating time, with a melt-down in the morning because Mommy turned on the TV instead of letting Anna do it herself, and a melt down in the afternoon because Daddy won't help Anna put on her socks. In addition to their unpredictable behavior, children are also prone to developing new fears – of animals, strangers, the dark, anything orange, or (in the case of one of my children) fuzz in the bathtub. For most children, these fears are temporary, and pass as the child adjusts to the world outside his doors; but for children who tend to be worriers, these fears can take root and significantly impact their lives.

By now, it should be clear that the years between two and five are a time of accelerated development, as the child moves out of the toddler phase and into childhood. Physically, the child is more coordinated and controlled in her movements, and becomes capable of controlling bowel and bladder functions. Cognitively, the child develops the ability to plan and think about the future, and form theories about how the world works. Emotionally, the child is struggling with competing wishes to be independent and be protected, and with managing the tumultuous feelings that accompany this internal conflict. These tasks demand a great deal from the child, and from the parents.

Despite the challenges of the early childhood years, most children weather the storms and sail into elementary school and calmer waters, at least until puberty rocks the boat. When children run aground during potty training, parents can feel like they have been shipwrecked on a deserted island. Friends, relatives, and even pediatricians may give well-intentioned advice about discipline, diet, exercise, the merits of diapers, pull-ups, and underpants. Parents try everything and if nothing works, they are forced to watch helplessly as their child suffers the consequences of chronic withholding and constipation, and their family life is held hostage by the child's problem.

Encopresis is not a common topic of conversation at playgroup or the preschool picnic. There is little information available to parents, and the few resources that exist tend to focus on behavioral treatments (i.e. rewards and punishments for using the potty). In my experience, these techniques have a place in the treatment of encopresis; however, there are many children who do not respond to rewards and punishment, no matter how wonderful or terrible.

So what is it that drives otherwise healthy children to avoid the potty like the plague or hold in their stool until they look as if they might explode?

CHAPTER 3

THE PSYCHOLOGY OF ENCOPRESIS

Carla and Lenore illustrate the more severe end of the spectrum when it comes to dealing with encopresis; but they are not unusual. Some children with encopresis potty train more or less successfully, but continue to soil. Others, like Lenore, never potty train, leaving their parents confused and frustrated. What is it that makes some children so resistant to potty training, while others put on the Spiderman underpants and never look back? Why do some children, who seem to be toilet trained, still soil their underpants on a regular basis?

Parents often think their children refuse to use the potty because they are willful, attention-seeking, or lazy. While some encopretic children may possess these characteristics, so do most children at one time or another. There are many ways a child can assert his will, get attention, or avoid work that do not require him to endure intense physical discomfort, social ostracism, and the continual disapproval and wrath of all of the adults in his life.

There must be something pretty powerful driving encopretic children to hold in their stools until their bellies are distended and cramping, and they are unable to play or eat. What could be so compelling that children will risk all manner of punishments administered by parents and teachers, and being called "poopy pants" by other children? I will let the children I have worked with tell you:

> Sarah believes that her bones and blood will come out with her poop.
>
> Marko thinks parts of his body can fall off anytime, and poop feels a lot like part of his body.
>
> Sam is afraid that his painful poops are tearing his body apart.
>
> Jenny worries that a snake will swim up the pipe into the toilet and bite her on the bottom while she sits there.

Take a moment to imagine whether you would be willing to poop on the toilet if you were convinced that one of these fates awaited you. Would a popsicle or an extra TV show, or even a spanking if you refuse, persuade you to try it? For many children with encopresis, holding onto their poop is a matter of life or death! It is *fear* that makes children willing to face severe physical discomfort, the anger of their parents, and ridicule from peers, rather than let a single nugget of stool fall into that potty.

But wait – maybe your child is one of those children who are perfectly happy to poop every day, even several times a day.....as long as it's not in the potty. Your child has no problem depositing his poop in a pull-up, diaper, or his underpants. In fact, sometimes you might wish he would stop pooping for awhile so you could get a break from cleaning up poopy messes! What's going on with these kids?

Some of these children, like Jenny, have fears about the potty or toilet being dangerous. The toilet is particularly threatening to a small child teetering on the edge of a large hole, which could suck her in and whisk her away with a roar at any time; or, equally horrifying, the large hole might conceal some terrible creature in its depths, which could swim out and grab the child in a very vulnerable spot! For children with a fear of the toilet, the simple, if temporary, fix is to let them poop on a potty chair – no water, no roaring, no hidden monsters. Several sessions of playtime with the toilet, when the child can flush things down and examine how the toilet works, may be enough to help these children conquer their fears.

Relatively few of the children I have worked with are afraid of the toilet. When children refuse to use the potty, it is usually because they are frightened by the sensation of the stool falling out of their bodies. The feeling that they are losing some vital part of themselves is heightened when the stool drops into the potty or toilet. Pooping in pull-ups or underpants is not as terrifying, because the poop remains in contact with their bodies. Once the deed is done, they may be happy to have the mess cleaned up and flushed away. It is not that their poops are so precious to them; it is rather that the moment of separation is deeply disturbing to these children.

For the majority of children who walk through the door to my office, accompanied by their frantic parents, pooping is a very scary activity that is best avoided until the last possible moment. So, how is it that some children develop such deep fears of a natural bodily process?

Most of the young children who come to see me (keep in mind these are children who have not responded to standard medical and behavioral therapies) have one or more of the following characteristics:

1. A history of constipation, reflux, or other gastrointestinal problems.
2. A family history of anxiety or other mental health disorders.
3. Sensory Integration Disorder.
4. Attention Deficit/Hyperactivity Disorder.

5. A history of serious health problems either for the child or a member of the immediate family.

6. Chronic physical conditions (other than constipation) that require medical intervention.

Encopresis is usually (but not always) triggered by an event which is traumatic to the child, even if it doesn't seem like a big deal to an adult. The most common trigger is a painful bowel movement. It is not just that it hurts; it is also associated with injury in the child's mind. A vicious cycle is begun when the child, who is trying to avoid a repeat of this experience, tries to hold in his or her stool. This results in more constipation, and more painful stools.

Other triggers might be an injury, illness, or surgery, a death in the family, or the birth of a sibling. Any event which makes the young child worried about the safety of his or her body, or is particularly stressful, can contribute to the development of encopresis.

Earlier I talked about how children normally pass through a stage of development when they become quite concerned about the integrity and safety of their bodies. This phase usually resolves as children accrue experiences which reinforce the strength and resilience of their bodies, and develop the cognitive skills to understand how their bodies work.

Many children with encopresis who don't respond to medical treatment have not been able to master their fears about their bodies. They feel vulnerable and anxious that serious injury awaits them around every corner. As they have told you, they worry that pooping will lead to injury or loss of body parts. Some of these children have anxiety disorders, and encopresis is one of the symptoms. They may go on to worry about monsters, robbers, taking tests, speaking in public, or flying in airplanes. Fortunately, there are many successful treatment options for anxiety disorder, including play therapy for young children, and talk therapy, cognitive-behavioral therapy, and medication for older children and adults. That's the good news. The bad news is that anxiety disorder is not always easy to diagnose in young children. Parents who have a child who refuses to use the potty may see a willful, controlling, emotional terrorist rather than a terrified tot.

Anxiety: Part of the Human Condition

It is part of being human to suffer from anxiety. We are biologically programmed to be on the look-out for danger, and ready to fight or flee when threatened. We would be foolish not to feel anxious when we step into the street and see the crosstown bus bearing down on us. Anxiety becomes a problem for some people when their brains perceive danger where there is none. They find themselves always in a state of red alert, expecting disaster to strike at any moment.

People develop characteristic ways of responding to overwhelming anxiety. Some take the fight approach, and become irritable, belligerent, or overbearing. Others take the flight approach, and stay in the house, stick to rigid routines, and avoid unfamiliar situations.

It's the same for young children, except they are less concerned with appearing crazy. Some children respond to feeling threatened by throwing epic tantrums, complete with kicking, hitting, and biting. Others break into hysterical sobbing at the drop of a hat. Then there are the anxious children who resist leaving the house, refuse to participate in new activities, and hide behind mom when asked to give granny a kiss. Anxious children protect themselves by trying to control their environments so that they feel comfortable. Routine has a special magic for many anxious children, and any deviation from the magic routine results in a melt-down. Put it all together and an anxious child can appear willful, stubborn, aggressive, uncooperative, rude, AND they won't poop on the potty. Dealing with an anxious child is not a recipe for feeling like a successful parent! Once parents realize that their child's obnoxious behavior is a sign of significant distress, and not the beginnings of a career criminal or politician, they are able to approach the situation in a more empathic, helpful way. Encopresis, while it may seem willful, stubborn, and defiant, is often an early symptom of anxiety in young children.

Trauma and Encopresis

Parents often ask if encopresis is the result of trauma. One of the first encopretic children I worked with was an eight-year-old boy. His mother was convinced that his soiling was a sign that a male relative was molesting him. I never found any evidence of sexual abuse, but I did find plenty of evidence of severe anxiety and anger over his parents' divorce. Over the years many parents have brought their children to see me with the fear that encopresis is related to sexual abuse. Sexual abuse is traumatic for children, and it fits with the theory that feeling physically vulnerable can trigger encopresis in some children; however in my practice I have never seen a child with encopresis who was sexually abused. This doesn't mean that those children are not out there, but it does indicate that there are many other types of trauma that are more common that can trigger encopresis.

Trauma makes children feel vulnerable and helpless. While children who are anxious worry that bad things will happen, children who have endured traumatic events know for certain that bad things happen. The majority of children that I treat for encopresis who have a history of trauma have suffered an injury or significant illness. The list includes severe feeding problems requiring feeding tubes, birth defects requiring surgeries, cancer, eye/ear/nose/ or throat problems, severe gastric reflux, and injuries which required hospitalizations or surgeries. These children have ample reasons to be worried about the safety and integrity of their bodies. Usually these traumatic events occur when children are very young, and lack the language or cognitive development to process what is happening to them. Adults often think that children don't remember early experiences, and it's true that they can't tell the story of what happened to them before they had language; however, these experiences remain in the memory as emotional states of fear and pain which can be triggered at any time. Children who have endured such trauma are also left with a general impression that their bodies are not dependable or safe. Early experiences of physical vulnerability can become tangled with normal developmental concerns about body safety, and cause some children to begin withholding stools in an effort to keep their bodies in one piece.

CHAPTER 4

OTHER CONDITIONS THAT CONTRIBUTE TO ENCOPRESIS

What about children with encopresis who have never completely potty trained, and for whom no particular triggering event can be identified? This group often includes children with sensory integration disorder, attentional problems, or poor internal proprioception. Anxiety may or may not accompany these conditions.

Sensory Integration Disorder

There is a good deal of information available to parents about sensory integration disorder, so I will not address it in detail; but I will provide the following example of how sensory integration problems can play a role in toileting difficulties:

James was never an easy baby. He cried lustily at birth, and rarely let up for the first few months of life. The only way his mother, Nancy could comfort him was to swaddle him tightly in a blanket and rock him vigorously. He breastfed well, but refused to take a bottle or a pacifier. He screamed whenever he was undressed or bathed or had his diaper changed. Nancy had fair warning when a diaper change was imminent because James would begin fussing and flailing his arms and legs several minutes before his little face turned red and he began to wail. Sometimes if Nancy flexed James' knees up to his chest it seemed to help, but pooping was always an ordeal.

As James grew, he resisted the transition to baby food, and then to solid food. By the time James was three, he ate only plain noodles and chicken nuggets. Nancy and James' father, Dave, worried about malnutrition. Dave put his foot down and made James sit at the table until he tried a bite of a new food. This led to protracted temper tantrums by both James and Dave. Mealtimes were a nightmare unless James got what he wanted.

Getting dressed was almost as bad. James wanted to wear his pajamas all day. When Nancy insisted that he dress so they could leave the house, James acted as if his clothing were made of barbed wire. He finally agreed to wear one pair of old sweatpants and two hand-me-down tee-shirts. Socks were unbearable, so James wore Crocs with no socks even in the dead of winter.

Dave's and Nancy's attempts to take James on fun outings usually backfired. He became hysterical at the circus because it was too noisy and it smelled bad. At the beach, he howled because the sand was scratchy. He couldn't go sledding with the neighbors because he refused to wear a jacket or mittens. James seemed happiest sitting on his favorite blanket in his favorite chair playing with his cars and trains.

When James showed no interest in potty training by the age of three, his parents were not worried. They knew that boys sometimes trained closer to four years old. The fact that James continued to whine and fuss when he felt a bowel movement coming on was of more concern. James complained that his stomach hurt, and curled up in a fetal position when he felt the urge to poop. Nancy coaxed him to relax and let the poop out, but James went rigid and moaned until the urge passed. Occasionally

James would suddenly looked panicked, run to crouch behind his favorite chair, and emerge with a stinky pull-up. He always denied that he had pooped, and resisted cleaning up until sufficient threats or incentives had been applied. At four-and-a-half, Nancy and Dave took James to see a pediatric gastroenterologist, who did various tests and diagnosed James with encopresis. Since there was no physical cause for James' soiling, the doctor told his parents that the causes of his problem were emotional, and referred James to a child psychologist. The psychologist asked Nancy and Dave about James' developmental history, and quickly surmised that James suffered from sensory integration disorder.

The psychologist explained that James' senses were extremely heightened so that every sensory perception - touch, taste, smell, sound - could be amplified to the point of discomfort or even pain. His day was a barrage of sensory information that was often unpleasant and overwhelming. Much of this sensory assault came from the environment around James, but some of his unpleasant sensations were internal. When James' digestive system geared up for elimination, the sensations of his colon contracting, the stool pressing on his anus causing the urge to defecate, and the passage of the stool through his anus were frighteningly intense and sometimes painful for James. It was no wonder that he resisted bowel movements, and when he couldn't contain them, resisted sitting on a cold, hard potty seat, preferring the secure, familiar environs of his favorite chair.

Because sensory integration disorder makes children hyper-aware of their bodies, it can heighten anxiety about whether their bodies are okay. Their bodies certainly don't feel okay much of the time. This worry contributes to their resistance to potty training because letting go of their stools feels like it is hurting their bodies.

Sensory integration problems are not always as severe as they were in James' case. There is a wide spectrum, from children who are picky about food or clothing to children who are constantly miserable and distracted by the intensity of the sensations that assault them all day long. Many children with sensory integration disorder have no difficulties with potty training; but for some children sensory issues can play a major role in the development of encopresis.

ADHD

Sean was the youngest of three boys. From the day he was born, he had no choice but to be an easy-going, go with the flow kind of guy. As an infant, he rarely fussed, ate whatever was put in front of him, and was happiest when he was crawling or toddling after his older brothers. His mother, Rita, was concerned that Sean slept less that her other boys. She often heard him talking cheerfully in his crib hours after bedtime, and was frequently awakened at dawn by Sean calling for her. He gave up his nap before he turned two. Sean's father, Sam, enjoyed his active, fearless son, and assured Rita that he had never needed much sleep either. By the time he could walk, Sean was into everything, could climb like a monkey, and was quick as a mongoose. Rita regularly found him teetering on the backs of chairs, dancing on tables, and attempting to scale the bookcase in the study. Sean incurred the wrath of his brothers by breaking their toys, knocking over their Lego creations, and scribbling on their homework papers. It was hard to stay angry with Sean for long because his mayhem never seemed deliberate, and his sunny disposition lit up the room.

When Sean started pre-school, his teachers enjoyed his personality, but found his activity level problematic in the classroom. He couldn't sit still for circle time or stories, lost interest in most activities before he had completed them, and made messes wherever he went. When his classmates displeased him, Sean was likely to shove them out of the way or hit. Then there were the accidents. Sean pooped or peed himself during school on a daily basis. In order to be in the three-year-old classroom, children were supposed to be potty trained; however, the pre-school director liked Rita and Sam, and had enjoyed having Sean's brothers at the school, so she quietly made an exception and let Sean join the other threes. Now she was worried that she would have to ask Sean to withdraw from the school. The teachers were weary of changing his soiled pull-ups, and the other parents were becoming aware of the problem and beginning to grumble about sanitary concerns. Rita was mortified. She was pretty sure Sean was hyper-active. Her brother had ADHD, and Sean acted the same way; but she couldn't understand why Sean had so much trouble with potty-training. He had a few accidents at home, but willingly went to the potty if she reminded him and was thrilled to get an M&M afterwards. She tried rewarding Sean for clean and dry days at school. At first it seemed her strategy was working, as Sean had a string of clean, dry days. Before long, though, the accidents began again. Now Rita was angry - she knew Sean could do it, and she thought he just wouldn't make the effort. She tried punishing him when he had an accident, but that only made them both frustrated and angry. Finally, at Sean's four year check-up, the pediatrician advised Rita to take Sean to a child psychiatrist.

Sean met the criteria for encopresis, but he didn't fit the usual picture of an encopretic child. He wasn't constipated, he didn't seem to be anxious, he willingly went in the potty when asked, so what was the problem?

The psychiatrist explained to Rita and Sam that a diagnosis of ADHD is difficult to make in a child as young as Sean. Under the age of five, many conditions can cause children to be hyperactive, impulsive, and distractible. Given Sean's behavior and family history, ADHD could not be ruled out either. The psychiatrist thought it was possible that Sean was so distracted by the lively environment that he simple didn't pay attention to the signals his body was sending him. His body was telling

Sean that it was REALLY time to pee or poop, but Sean was distracted by playing dinosaur wars with the boys at school or riding his tricycle pell mell after his brothers on their bikes. By the time he realized that his body was talking to him, it was too late - his body had taken unilateral action without him.

At home, Rita had trained herself to remind Sean to use the potty at regular intervals, so he had fewer accidents. The teachers at school didn't issue reminders, and left to his own devices, Sean often missed his internal cues because he was paying attention to something more interesting.

The ability to attend to internal cues and carry out a plan of action before it's too late are critical skills for success on the potty. Children who have difficulties with attention and sustained focus can also have a tendency towards disorganization, poor planning, and procrastination. They may also have a hard time *shifting* attention from one task to another. If they are engaged in an enjoyable activity, it is a struggle for them to disengage and focus on something else. For children with ADHD, the "something else" may be getting to the potty on time.

But the Doctor Said There Is No Physical Cause...

When children are diagnosed with encopresis, it means that no physical cause has been found to explain their soiling; however, it is my observation that there are some children who do not suffer from an identifiable gastrointestinal disorder, but do have subtle physical conditions that make toilet training challenging. These include poor internal proprioception, weak muscle tone, and delays in motor skill development.

Poor Proprioception

Proprioception refers to the ability of the body to feel and interpret cues from the environment. When we walk barefoot across the lawn, our feet tell us whether the grass is long or short, soft or coarse, wet or dry, cool or warm. They let us know if the ground is uneven so that we can compensate and not fall down, and, ouch!, that Thomas the Tank Engine has been left in the grass again. We also receive signals from inside our bodies. Our stomach tells us when we need to eat or when we've eaten too much....again. Our bodies communicate when we are thirsty, tired, cold, or sick. As we discussed earlier, we also get signals when we need to use the toilet. Where children who have problems with attention don't listen to these signals soon enough, other children seem unable to hear the signals at all or to recognize what the signals mean.

Anna's parents brought her to my office when she was six-years-old because she was still having urine and bowel accidents. Her pediatrician thought Anna was expressing unconscious feelings about her adoption, or perhaps anger at her rather strict parents. Shelly and Rob adopted Anna from Russia when she was two. The first years of her life were spent in a Russian orphanage. There she spent most of the day in a crib. Although she wasn't treated unkindly, the staff was too overwhelmed to provide much attention, and fed, bathed, and changed Anna when they got around to it. When Shelly and Rob brought Anna home, she spoke only a few Russian words and she couldn't walk. Within six months, Anna was chattering away in English, and toddling on sturdy little legs. By the time she was four, Anna showed few signs of her early developmental delays other than general clumsiness and no signs that she was ready to potty train. Her parents figured Anna was still catching up, and didn't pressure her about the potty. When Anna turned five and still wasn't out of diapers, Shelly and Rob began to be concerned. Anna's doctors found nothing physically wrong, so Shelly and Rob stepped up their efforts at toilet training. Over the course of the next year, they tried every technique and trick they had ever heard of, but nothing worked - Anna continued to wet and soil. It was particularly infuriating when Shelly or Rob had just sat her on the toilet with no results, and ten minutes later Anna had an accident. The angrier Shelly and Rob became, the more sullen and uncooperative Anna became. Things were at an all-time low when the family came to see me.

It was many weeks before I could even mention Anna's "problem" without having her clam up or act like she hadn't heard me. She was an expert at avoiding and changing the subject; and no wonder, since the topic was usually accompanied by disapproval, anger, and punishment. Even worse was the shame Anna felt over her inability to control her body. She took to hiding her soiled clothing at the back of her closet, desperately wishing it would magically disappear before her mother found it and blew up at her. Even her doctor had give her a stern talking-to about hygiene and proper toileting technique. In Anna's experience, talking about her problem with the potty made her feel deeply incompetent and ashamed.

After many hours of playing with the animal families on the floor of my office, Anna began to trust that I wasn't going to ambush her with a potty lecture. Over time, I let her know about all the other children who had problems being in charge of their bodies that came to see me. Anna was amazed to hear that she was not alone with her problem. As we talked, I asked Anna how her body felt just before a pee or poop. Her puzzled look confirmed my hunch that Anna couldn't tell when she needed to go to the bathroom. Either her body wasn't sending good signals, or Anna wasn't able to recognize them.

Having seen the same situation with several children adopted from institutional orphanages, I formed a tentative hypothesis. Infants constantly experience massive amounts of input from inside and outside their bodies. At first they have no way to differentiate or identify these sensations. Babies either feel bad, or they feel good. It is only through interactions with caregivers that babies learn to identify what they are feeling. Normally, when baby has a bad feeling she cries. Someone hears her and comes to feed her. Now the bad feeling is gone. As this cycle is repeated over and over, the baby learns that a particular bad feeling is hunger, and milk makes it go away. Another sensation results in someone coming to change the baby's diaper, while cooing things like, "Look what a good poopy you did! Let's clean up that messy tushie!" Eventually baby recognizes the sensation of pooping. But suppose baby has bad feelings, cries, and no one comes to make the feelings go away. Feeding and changing take place on a schedule that has nothing to do with what the baby feels. Not only does baby fail to have the experiences that teach her how to tell one feeling from another, her feelings have no context at all. Eventually baby ignores her feelings just like her caretakers do, and learns to wait passively for care.

Whether this happened to Anna, or there was another reason for her lack of awareness of her bodily sensations, it was apparent that she simply didn't know when it was time to get up and go. Urine and bowel accidents were as much of an unpleasant surprise to her as to her parents.

Deficits in Strength and Coordination

Children with low muscle tone or delayed motor skills may be prone to constipation because they lack the strength or coordination to efficiently push out stools. Chronic constipation can lead to encopresis when liquid stool seeps around a solid mass in the colon, causing frequent soiling. Occasionally these children end up in my office because the connection between their physical challenges and encopresis has not been recognized. Unless there are clearly mental health issues present, I do not believe that therapy is necessary for children in this category, so I will not discuss their treatment in depth.

In my opinion, good medical treatment is vital for these children. Maintaining soft stools and providing extra stimulation to defecate can be helpful to prevent constipation. Biofeedback is a possible option for children who have insufficient strength or coordination to push out stools. Often these children are receiving occupational therapy because their motor skills are impaired. It is important to make the occupational therapist aware of any toileting problems so that attention can be directed towards core muscle strengthening, and developing body awareness of how it feels to push stool out of the anus.

Just as there are many factors that are involved in creating toileting problems, there are many interventions that need to be part of a comprehensive treatment plan. In the next section, I will talk about the three key areas that need to be assessed and addressed: physical health, behavior, and emotions of both the child and the parents.

PART II

TREATMENT STRATEGIES

CHAPTER 5

PARENTAL SELF-CARE

Medical students are told, "In an emergency, first take your own pulse." A hyperventilating med student is not in any condition to respond to a gunshot wound. It's not so different for parents of encopretic children. You've been through a lot! You are probably frustrated, angry, embarrassed, fed up, and feeling like a terrible parent because your child is still having accidents, when your sister's kids have been potty trained since they were six months old! It's not supposed to be this hard! So, please listen to me when I tell you: THIS IS NOT YOUR FAULT! And feel free to tell your sister and your mother-in-law that I said so. However, do take the time to check in with yourself.

How is your physical health? Are you modeling good self-care for your child? I know you will probably roll your eyes when I say this, as busy parents often feel they have no time for themselves; but do your best to eat a healthy diet, stay active, and get enough rest. Give yourself permission to let go of activities and commitments that are not essential or rewarding. Your child will not suffer if he doesn't play pee-wee soccer, or if you decline the honor of serving as the PTA treasurer. If you are stressed and overwhelmed, it will be difficult for you to find the patience and focus to help your child conquer encopresis.

Take a clear-eyed look at your behavior. Are you in control c̄ self? Is your response to your child's problem proactive or reactive? ... other words, are you thinking of ways you can help your child master her toileting problems, or are you reacting to each accident on auto-pilot? Is the way you are behaving helping or hurting the situation? It is so easy to find yourself locked in a power struggle with your child, or in an angry, punitive cycle. Neither is helpful in conquering encopresis.

Get a grip on your emotions. Identify what you are feeling about the situation and how your feelings influence your response to your child. Do you feel angry and punitive, frustrated and hopeless, incompetent and guilty? Whatever you feel will be transmitted to your child. Children are practically telepathic when it comes to reading their parents' emotions. Your negative emotions, while understandable, are not helping the situation. Your child needs a hopeful, empathic, enthusiastic cheerleader on his or her team, who can model the way to tackle challenges with patience and persistence. See this as an opportunity to teach your child a life lesson that goes far beyond the bathroom! If you aren't able to reprogram your emotional response, it is essential to find out what has you trapped in a negative feedback loop. Individual counseling or psychotherapy is the most effective and efficient way to learn how to change your emotional responses so that you can be more helpful to your child. This investment will pay dividends throughout your parenting career. Much better to work on yourself now so you can be a better parent, rather than wait until your child is 17, fed up with you, and has the keys to the car.

CHAPTER 6

TAKING A TEAM APPROACH

Now that you've taken your own pulse, it's time to focus on your child. Take your child to a pediatric gastroenterologist to rule out any physical causes for constipation and soiling. Chronic constipation can lead to a condition called megacolon, where the colon becomes stretched from holding large amounts of stool. Children with this condition struggle even more with regular elimination because of the loss of tone in their colons. Many lose the ability to feel when they need to have a bowel movement due to stretching in the rectum. This is a potentially serious problem which must be addressed before permanent damage is done.

An assessment by a pediatric gastroenterologist will determine the best course of medical treatment for your child. Each child is different, and may require a different regimen to help reestablish regular elimination. Pediatricians are very good at treating routine constipation, but few have much experience with the treatment of encopresis. Most pediatric gastroenterologists have treated hundreds of children with constipation and encopresis. Sometimes medical treatment alone can get your child back on track. This may not be pleasant for your child, but it is necessary.

Just as I refer patients to the gastroenterologist (from now on referred to as the GI, for both our sakes), for medical treatment, many pediatric GIs recognize that there is often a behavioral and/or emotional component to encopresis, and refer patients to a therapist like me. Other parents hear about me from teachers or friends. If you are unable to get a referral to a good child therapist, you will have to do some research on your own. The internet and your insurance company's provider list are not necessarily the best source for finding a competent therapist, although there may be good clinicians in both places. The problem is that there will also be therapists who will not be competent to treat encopresis both on the web and on your insurance list, and you will spend hours trying to sort the wheat from the chaff. Better to ask people you know and respect for the names of good child therapists, or call your local medical center. If there are names that you hear more than once, start by calling them. Even if these clinicians can't help you, they will likely know the names of other good therapists in the area.

Unfortunately, young children represent an underserved population in the mental health field. Only a small minority of therapists (even child therapists) treat children under the age of six, and are trained in play therapy. An even smaller number of therapists have much experience treating encopresis. Ideally, you will find a clinician who meets all of these criteria; however, a well-trained, competent, experienced child therapist can help you even if encopresis is not their speciality. While degrees and credentials are important, more is not always better. There are many wonderful therapists who have Master's degrees in Social Work or Professional Counseling who do work that is as good or better than many Ph.D.s or M.D.s; however, the best trained therapist will have a graduate degree in the mental health field and will be licensed by the state in which you live.

So, you have made an appointment with a therapist who has been enthusiastically recommended by your child's old pre-school teacher, your pediatrician, and your neighbor with the garden gnomes out front.

What can you expect on that first visit? Different therapists do things different ways, but I'll tell you what I do, so you have a general idea of what to look for. When you make contact with me, the first thing I do is schedule a comprehensive assessment of your child.

I will meet with parents for the first hour, without your child present. During this meeting, I get a detailed developmental history for your child, including an in-depth description of the problem. I ask when the encopretic symptoms began; whether your child is constipated or withholding; whether there is soiling, and if so, how often; has your child ever used the potty; where does elimination occur - in a diaper, underpants, on the floor; whether your child tells you when he has soiled; whether your child demonstrates awareness of the urge to defecate. Does she tell a caretaker she needs to poop, or run behind the couch, or poop with no warning in the middle of daily activities? Is there is a particular time of day your child is likely to poop? I have more questions about poop than anyone you've ever met! Understanding a child's behavior helps me decide where to begin trying to change it, and also gives me clues into the emotional reasons for a child's difficulties.

The initial meeting is also a time for you to express your concerns and ask questions. In working with any therapist, whether for yourself or your child, it's important that you feel comfortable with the therapist's personality and style. A good therapist is not offended if you decide to seek help elsewhere because the fit isn't right. You may be seeing a lot of this person for a long time, so choosing a clinician who is a good match for you and your child is crucial.

If we decide to work together, I will have three play sessions with your child to perform a developmental assessment and see how your child responds to me. Then the adults will meet again to talk about a treatment plan for your child. Sometimes, I can give parents suggestions to try at home before committing to weekly play therapy; but more often, I recommend weekly play therapy for your child and regular parent meetings. The play therapy is to address the emotional factors that are contributing to your child's encopresis. Parent meetings are for us to create strategies to change your child's toileting behavior.

I am telling you what would happen if you came to my practice so that you can get a feel for how the therapeutic process begins. Other therapists may approach the assessment differently. The point is to learn as much as we can about your child so that we can decide how to provide the most effective treatment for him or her.

CHAPTER 7

KNOW YOUR CHILD

Potty Readiness

Before I discuss strategies that you can try at home, let's break pooping down to a series of steps that must be mastered in order for children to use the toilet independently. First of all, your child must be able to feel and recognize the urge to defecate. In addition, your child must be able to pay attention when she has the urge, and not be distracted by other activities. If your child seems surprised by producing a poop in the middle of doing other things, he may have difficulty with one or both of these tasks. A child who runs behind the couch or into her closet to poop is demonstrating that she knows when she needs to have a b.m.

The next set of skills relate to access to the potty. Can your child make it to the potty in time? Is there a potty near by? Can your child pull down his own pants? If she is using the toilet, can she climb up onto the seat, and is it comfortable to sit there? Many children are afraid they will fall in the toilet, and are much more cooperative when there is a ring in the opening which fits their small bottoms. When sitting on the toilet, your child's feet may not touch the ground. Make sure there is a footstool for your child's feet to rest on. It makes him feel more secure and gives him something to push against.

If your child is capable of accessing the potty, but avoids it, she is probably anxious about the process. As I mentioned earlier, some kids are happy to poop in a pull-up or diaper so that they won't feel the feces dropping out of their bodies. Other children hold their poop in until they're ready to explode because they fear the bowel movement will hurt, or because the whole pooping process, from the first contractions of the colon to the stool exiting the anus, is miserable for them. Less commonly, there are kids who are deathly afraid of the potty, especially the big toilet. They worry that they will fall in and be flushed away, or that an awful creature will swim up the drain and bite them. Sometimes the noise of the flush is frightening. The anxiety needs to be conquered before your child will be able to participate in toilet training.

Finally, if your child seems willing and able to sit on the toilet, but isn't productive, she may be constipated, or have poor tone in her colon or muscles in general. A few children don't know how to engage their muscles in pushing the stool out. Medical treatment, occupational or physical therapy may be helpful in these situations.

Your Unique Child

At this point, it should be clear that not all encopretic children are alike. A therapeutic plan for a seven-year-old boy who soils daily in school, and has ADHD, oppositional/defiant disorder, and poor muscle tone will differ from a therapeutic plan for a four-year-old girl who screams when she is brought near the potty, will only poop in a diaper, and has sensory integration disorder. Although neither of these children is toilet trained, their encopresis is a symptom which is caused by other factors. Just as you want to determine whether your child's stomach ache is caused by a virus, lactose intolerance, or appendicitis, it's important to think about what is getting in the way of your child mastering proper toileting behavior. You know your child better than anyone. Which of the skills discussed above has your child not acquired? Which of the factors discussed in this book sound like they apply to your child? They are listed below. Perhaps you will identify other issues that might make toileting difficult for your child.

1. Anxiety
2. Trauma
3. Sensory Integration Disorder
4. ADHD
5. Low muscle tone
6. Inability to perceive or interpret internal proprioceptive cues.

Knowing which skills your child still needs to master, and which of the conditions listed above best describes your child, will aid you in deciding where and how to focus your efforts to help your child develop independent toileting skills.

CHAPTER 8

GENERAL TECHNIQUES

Taking each factor individually, I will discuss some strategies that might be helpful to your child, or that might inspire some strategies of your own. Before I do that, here are some parenting techniques that are good to keep in mind with any child diagnosed with encopresis:

1. Be on your child's team. Encopresis is not a problem your child is deliberately creating. He or she needs your help and understanding, not your condemnation.

2. Punishment, while appropriate in some child-rearing situations, does not work with encopresis. If it did, you would have fixed the problem long ago. Positively rewarding desired behavior works far more effectively.

3. On the other hand, don't make things too easy or pleasant for your child. Washing his little bottom with a warm cloth while singing songs to him doesn't provide much incentive to begin using the potty.

4. If your child is willing to cooperate (with or without a small incentive), establish daily potty sitting times. Some children need to be induced to sit on the potty by having something special to do while sitting that they aren't allowed to do any other time. Some clinicians disagree with me, and think activities on

the potty are too distracting and prevent children from concentrating on producing a poop. My experience has led me to believe that most children are more likely trying *not* to produce a poop when first introduced to potty sits, but a special activity while sitting establishes a positive association with the bathroom and the potty. Potty sits should occur two or three times a day for five to ten minutes after school, after meals, or any time your child is likely to produce a bowel movement. Don't drag your child to the potty kicking and screaming. This is not likely to result in positive associations.

5. Begin where your child is. If your child is terrified of the toilet, starting with toilet sits will probably not work well. Begin by helping your child master her fear of the toilet. When a child can't feel when he needs to poop, making a plan to reward him for pooping on the potty is premature. Working on recognizing internal sensations, and using a toileting schedule is a good place to start.

CHAPTER 9

THE THREE DOMAINS OF ENCOPRESIS

There is no "one size fits all" treatment for encopresis; however, good treatment usually addresses three areas simultaneously. The physical, behavioral, and emotional domains should all be included in an effective plan of attack. Physical problems may include constipation, poor muscle tone, and lack of sensation in the anus, among others, which make proper toileting difficult for a child. As children struggle with toileting, they adopt behaviors, such as withholding stool or toilet avoidance, to deal with their fear and frustration. The longer the problem continues, the more intense the negative emotions associated with toileting become for both children and parents. Since these three domains interact to create problems with the potty, a comprehensive plan that covers all three areas has the best chance of success.

The Physical Domain

I cannot stress enough that encopretic children need to be under the care of a physician who is experienced in treating the problem. Physical causes must be ruled out, and a medical regimen to treat constipation must be in place. Continued constipation can be harmful to a child's body, and causes painful stools, which reinforces a child's resistance to pooping in the potty.

The Behavioral Domain

There is a large body of research that shows that positive reinforcement plans are more effective than punishment when it comes to altering behavior. This is certainly true in the treatment of encopresis, when children are not pooping in their pants in a deliberate effort to be naughty. I will say a little bit about behavior plans, because if they are not implemented correctly, they won't work.

The purpose of a behavior plan in the treatment of encopresis is to motivate a child to learn good toileting habits. A good behavior plan has the following qualities:

1. It's simple to understand and follow. The father of a child in my practice devised a behavior plan that involved earning a certain number of points for different behaviors, which translated into minutes on the computer, but only up to a maximum of 30 minutes during the week, unless.......You get the idea. The child took one look at the plan and refused to have anything to do with it. Pick one behavior to focus on, and reward the child when he performs that behavior. Keep it simple!

2. Choose a behavior that your child can perform. If you try to reward a child for staying clean when she can't tell that she's soiled herself, you are setting her up for failure. Start where your child is now, and move step by step towards the end goal of independent toileting. If your child is hiding behind the couch to poop, reward him for pooping in the bathroom, and move on from there. Be sure each step along the way is thoroughly mastered before going to the next.

3. State the behavior in positive terms. Tell your child what behavior you want rather than what behavior you don't want. For example, say, "from now on, I'd like you to make your poops in the bathroom," rather than "no pooping behind the couch!"

4. Choose a reward that is motivating for your child, and that you can reliably provide. If the reward is too big, you won't be able to keep giving it. If the reward is too small, it won't be interesting to your child. In my experience, it's the rare child who is motivated by stickers. The reward can be a thing, such as a small toy or an M&M; an experience, like playing a game with Daddy or Mommy; or a privilege, like choosing a movie for the family to watch. Some children love a prize box; others get overwhelmed with too many choices. Be creative!

5. Establish a reinforcement schedule that is appropriate for your child's age and temperament. Young children need to be rewarded immediately every time they perform the target behavior in order for them to associate the behavior with the reward. If you delay, they move on and forget what they did that got your approval. Some older children can wait for gratification, but they still need to have something to mark their achievement. You might be able to set up a plan for a child over the age of seven that rewards them for every three poops in the potty, but they still need to get a ticket or a token each and every time, or keep a chart so they can track their progress.

6. Be consistent! The biggest problem families have with behavior plans is consistency. Life is busy, and children do not always perform target behaviors at convenient times; but you must make it a priority to follow the plan and reward on schedule.

7. Give it time. Parents often come to me after a week of trying a behavior plan and tell me it isn't working. New behaviors take time to develop, and this is not easy for your child. Try the plan consistently for at least 3 weeks. If you aren't seeing any progress by then, re-evaluate the plan and adjust as needed.

If you implement a behavior plan that is simple, appropriate, motivating, and consistent, and still get nowhere, it probably means that your child's anxiety level is too high for any reward to be effective. If she believes that pooping threatens her existence, she will not do it for any number of trips to Disney World. In that case, the behavior plan has to wait while you focus on reducing your child's level of anxiety.

The Emotional Domain

Anxiety, anger, shame, frustration, terror, and sadness are just some of the emotions children (and parents) may feel when dealing with encopresis. While these feelings are normal, they are not helpful. Negative emotions can cause us to behave in counter-productive ways. We may respond by becoming belligerent, oppositional, avoidant, withdrawn, or depressed. These reactions prevent us from facing problems with insight, clarity, empathy, and intelligence. It's important to help your child identify and deal with the feelings that *cause* encopresis - usually anxiety - and with the feelings *caused by* having encopresis. Parents also need to clarify and deal with the feelings they have about their child's condition before they can be helpful participants in their child's recovery. This is where a good therapist can provide support and guidance. Proper treatment provides a safe forum for expressing feelings, examining how feelings influence behavior, and developing healthier coping mechanisms.

Young children achieve these goals through participation in play therapy. Play is the medium through which children interact with the world. Babies learn about gravity and how to engage the attention of adults by dropping their spoons on the floor over and over. Toddlers learn about empathy, social behavior, and cause and effect when they take a toy from another child. As children get older, they learn about social roles, problem-solving, controlling emotions, and delaying gratification by playing make-believe games with peers.

Children express their thoughts and feelings more eloquently in play than in words. They explore feelings about their families and themselves by playing with the dollhouse. All of those fighting games with action figures or Pokemon express and help master fears about being strong and competent enough to survive in the big, scary world outside their front doors. Pushing Play Doh out of the Fun Factory is a metaphor - well, we all know what Play Doh is, metaphorically speaking.

A good play therapist guides children through the imaginary worlds they create in play, helps them master difficult emotions and challenging situations, and promotes the development of skills that serve them well when managing future challenges. Play therapists also provide support and guidance to parents, who are usually eager to help their children with their struggles. So, don't be concerned when you ask your child what he did with his therapist and he says, "we just played." He's actually working very hard.

CHAPTER 10

THE ANXIOUS POOPER

Let's check in with Lenore and Carla. Carla's fantasies of motherhood were shattered when she gave birth to her colicky, intense, anxious, strong-willed daughter. Lenore's panicky behavior when she got minor scrapes and cuts, and her fear of haircuts, doctors and dentists are indications that she is particularly worried about her body. She fears that her body is in danger of severe injury at all times. The very thought of someone touching her is enough to send her into orbit, especially if she could be stabbed with needles, have large fingers and sharp instruments stuffed into her mouth, or have any part of herself cut - even her hair! The feeling of feces dropping out of her body triggers panic in Lenore because it feels like she is losing parts of her internal organs. No amount of logic and factual information can convince Lenore otherwise. She tries her best to hold everything inside, but when she fails, pooping into a pull-up lessens the sensation of body parts falling out of her.

Raising a child like Lenore is a challenge. How can Carla feel like a good parent when her kid is constantly whining and complaining, or hysterical, and refusing to potty train in addition? It's enough to make Carla want to hop in her time machine, go back to high school, and remain a virgin for the rest of her life. Since that's not an option, how can Carla survive parenthood, and more importantly, how can she help Lenore master her anxiety about her body?

Fortunately, Carla took her doctor's advice and took Lenore to be evaluated by a child therapist. After hearing Carla's story, the therapist empathized with the sadness, anger, and guilt Carla felt. Anxious temperaments are hereditary, so while Carla's genes may be partly responsible, she can hardly beat herself up about that. The therapist helped Carla understand that Lenore's difficult behavior was not a response to Carla's mothering, but a reaction to an internal state of high alert that bordered on panic at all times. When Carla tiptoed around on eggshells for fear of upsetting Lenore, she reinforced Lenore's anxiety that the world was a dangerous place. (See, even Mommy is worried about what will happen next!) With treatment, Carla began to find a better balance between coddling Lenore and overwhelming her. Realizing that Lenore's meltdowns were not the result of her poor parenting skills freed Carla to be more empathic to Lenore's reactivity and fear, so that she could provide Lenore with support, and not cave in to Lenore's irrational worries. The therapist insisted that Lenore's father, Rich, participate in the parent meetings along with Carla. It was important that he know how to support both Lenore and Carla, and be able to take over so that Carla had breaks. Rich found that his confidence in his parenting increased, while Carla was less drained by Lenore's needs. With the help of the therapist, Carla and Rich learned strategies to help Lenore cope with anxiety and soothe herself when she began to get panicky.

While the relationship between Carla and Lenore improved, Lenore's potty skills remained unchanged. With a foundation of growing trust and affection between mother and daughter, Carla and the therapist began addressing Lenore's fears about her body. In play therapy, Lenore and the therapist made snakes out of Play Doh, chopped them up and threw them into a bucket. Lenore demanded that the therapist retrieve the pieces, while her fingers were attacked by alligators that lived in the bucket. Through the play, Lenore expressed her fears about injury to her body by turning the attackers on the therapist. After the therapist had survived hundreds of alligator bites, Lenore began to feel brave enough to put her own fingers into the bucket. "The alligators don't bite me - they only bite YOU!" Lenore cried triumphantly.

As Lenore was conquering her fear of the potty in play therapy, Carla was implementing strategies at home to help Lenore learn good toileting habits. The therapist recommended some books for Carla to read to Lenore about overcoming fears about the potty, and about how her body works. Lenore demanded to hear the books over and over, as she slowly began to understand that her poop was not a body part, but was old food that needed to come out. In addition, Carla got a special doll for Lenore to potty train. Lenore loved to take the doll into the bathroom and sit her on the potty. One day, Carla stopped by the bathroom door to hear Lenore tell her doll, "Don't worry, it doesn't hurt."

Carla and the therapist also established a behavior plan to encourage Lenore to learn new toileting behaviors. Since Lenore didn't want anything to do with the bathroom, except when taking a bath, Carla began by letting Lenore play in the bathroom. Lenore played with water in the sink, smeared shaving cream in the tub, and had flushing parties with Carla where they sent bits of toilet paper and the occasional Tic Tac swirling into the unknown. As Lenore associated the bathroom with more enjoyable activities, Carla began asking Lenore to go into the bathroom to poop in her pull-up. When Lenore successfully made her poops in the bathroom, Carla rewarded her by letting her choose a prize from the treasure box. Soon, Lenore was leading Carla into the bathroom whenever she needed to make a poop. Together they emptied the pull-up into the toilet and sent the poop off to Poopyland by singing the "Bye Bye Poopy" song.

Once Lenore was securely having b.m.s in the bathroom, Carla established times for sitting on the potty twice a day. Lenore did not have to produce a poop, but she was required to sit for five minutes in order to get her prize. To sweeten the deal, Carla let Lenore play with a special, new toy while she sat on the potty. Lenore never got to have the toy any other time. Carla chose well, and soon Lenore was difficult to get off of the potty. In the meantime, Lenore was continuing to master her fears about her body in therapy. As the weeks progressed and Lenore was still not producing poops in the potty, Carla was beginning to become discouraged. The therapist pointed out that Lenore now allowed Carla to cut her nails, and take her for a haircut without a meltdown. Progress was being made in other areas, and the therapist was confident that the toileting would progress as well.

Because of Lenore's flair for the dramatic, Carla made Lenore a beautiful crown and princess gown. Carla told Lenore that when she became the ruler of her body, and made her poops go in the potty, the crown and dress would be hers to wear after every poop. Lenore begged for the dress and crown, but Carla remained firm. Lenore threw a tantrum. Carla calmly told her, "I see that you aren't quite big enough for a beautiful princess dress, but I'm sure you will be soon." After a week of intermittent pleading and raging did not get Lenore the dress and crown, Carla was stunned to hear Lenore call from the bathroom one morning, "Mommy! Come look what I did!" There was much rejoicing as Carla and Lenore sent Lenore's poopy from the potty to Poopyland. Carla crowned Princess Lenore, who remained in her royal regalia until bedtime. Daddy was appropriately impressed with his little princess when he came home from work, and Princess Lenore was allowed to be the ruler of dessert that evening. The next morning, Lenore pooped in her pull-up. "So much for happy endings," thought Carla; however, she remained calm and matter-of-fact. Lenore was quite disappointed that she was not a princess that day. "Well, maybe tomorrow," said Carla. Soon Lenore was a princess more days than not, and eventually even the princess dress and crown were forgotten as pooping in the potty became the routine.

Lenore conquered her fear of pooping in the potty. Carla and Rich were thrilled. They were able to finish up their work with the therapist, with the understanding that Lenore might have other bumps in the road as she learned to deal with her anxious temperament. While the family was glad to know that the therapist's door was always open, they all felt that they had gained confidence and insight into how to work together to help Lenore stay on her developmental track.

CHAPTER 11

THE SENSITIVE POOPER

Children with Sensory Integration Disorder, such as James, share much in common with anxious children. Both may fear that something injurious is happening to their bodies when they have a bowel movement; but where Lenore worried that something bad *might* happen, for James it felt as if something bad *was* happening. Because of his sensory sensitivities, pooping was a traumatic experience. His whole body felt as if it were in a state of upheaval that felt frightening and overwhelming to James. Trying to convince James that letting the poop come out will feel better than holding it in was not an easy task. Even after James was being treated medically so that his poops were soft, and not painful, he disliked the internal sensation of his colon contracting and the urge to push out his stool. His agitation was so great that there was no way to get him to the potty.

James and his parents also benefited from working with a child therapist to help James learn coping skills to calm himself when he was upset, and help his parents gradually shape his toileting behavior. In addition, James saw an occupational therapist, who showed James and his parents various techniques to keep his body more comfortable and relaxed, and helped reduce the intensity of James' sensitivities. Once Dave understood the nature of James' difficulties, he stopped trying to force James to engage in activities that were distressing for him. Dave even signed up for a yoga class that he and James could attend together, so that they could both learn some relaxing breathing and movements. When Dave came home from work, James was waiting for him to practice deep breathing, muscle relaxation, and meditation. Dave was pleasantly surprised, by the way, to find that his blood pressure was lower than it had been in years at his next physical exam.

Now that their relationship had improved, James was willing to accept his father's suggestion that they practice relaxation in the bathroom. They found a meditation CD for children that led them through a visualization exercise where they imagined their favorite place. James was so pleased to have his father's attention that he willingly participated while sitting on the toilet (lid closed) while Dave sat on a stool nearby. When James began to look like he was gearing up for a pooping episode, Dave or Nancy would encourage him to practice relaxing in the bathroom rather than in his favorite chair. When James was able to stay in the bathroom, he got to pick a toy car to add to his collection.

Nancy found a comfortable seat for the toilet that had a footrest and handles to hold onto, where James could perch securely while listening to his meditation CD. At first, he sat on his "throne" with his diaper on. When he was able to poop in his diaper while sitting on the throne, he was declared "Poopy King," and was able to command Nancy or Dave to do the "Poopy Dance." Although performing the Poopy Dance was somewhat embarrassing when guests were present, it seemed a small price to pay for James' cooperation on the toilet. James was so delighted to be able to command his parents to act silly that he sometimes pooped twice in one day.

While Dave and Nancy were thrilled that James was at least sitting on the toilet and letting his poop out, he still steadfastly refused to take off his diaper. Instead of struggling with him over the diaper, Nancy left the diaper on James, but began cutting small holes in it. At first the holes were so tiny James could barely see them. When James was ready to "graduate" to a bigger hole, he received a diploma and got to make a graduation speech to his attentive parents. One day, a small nugget of poop escaped from the diaper and fell into the toilet. The family celebrated with a trip to the ice cream parlor after dinner.

It was a long time before James was ready to give up the security of having the diaper wrapped around him, but eventually the hole in the diaper was big enough to allow most of his poop to fall into the toilet. As James grew, his sensitivities to environmental and internal stimuli grew less acute, and his skill at managing his comfort level increased. Although he never wore jeans, and always preferred macaroni and cheese to Szechuan noodles, James was comfortable in his own skin.

CHAPTER 12

THE OBLIVIOUS POOPER

Anxiety played a major role in preventing both Lenore and James from toilet training smoothly. Lenore was afraid of hurting her body, and James feared the feelings that accompanied a bowel movement. Play therapy was instrumental in helping them master their anxiety and overcome their encopresis. With children such as Sean, who has attentional difficulties, and Anna, who has poor internal cues, play therapy may have a different role. Neither Sean nor Anna is particularly anxious about pooping on the potty - they are unaware that they have to go until it's too late. They know they are failing at a major developmental task that other children seem to master easily; but they don't know why or how to fix it. This kind of failure can arouse a great deal of shame and self-doubt. Play therapy may be necessary to help Sean and Anna process these painful feelings, and rebuild self-esteem.

A therapist can also help parents develop accommodations and support strategies while their children are learning to listen to the cues their bodies are sending. Establishing a schedule of potty sitting is important for children who don't recognize when they need to use the bathroom. Sean's mother got a watch with a timer for Sean to wear to school. Every two hours the timer reminded Sean to try going to the bathroom. At home, Rita instituted three times during the day for Sean to sit on the potty and try to poop. She noticed that he tended to poop either after school, or after dinner, so Sean sat on the potty at those times, and in the morning (just in case). When Sean resisted sitting, Rita didn't fight with him; she simply refused to let him engage in other activities until he sat. Sitting cooperatively earned Sean a reward, whether he pooped or not. Rita engaged Sean's brothers to help by agreeing to play whatever game Sean chose if he actually produced a poop in the potty. Sean was used to following his big brothers around, so being able to choose an activity with them was a rare and precious privilege. Sean tried very hard to pay attention to his body; and soon the family got used to jumping out of the way when Sean came charging to the bathroom. Sometimes he didn't make it time, but his accidents grew less frequent. By the time he was five-years-old, Sean was diagnosed with ADHD, which surprised no one. Although he faced other challenges, by then, his accidents were a thing of the past.

Like Sean, Anna didn't recognize when she needed to go to the bathroom. Her internal signals had no meaning for her. Scheduled toilet sits were a key component of Anna's treatment plan, since she couldn't rely on physical cues. She also had a watch with a timer that reminded her to use the bathroom at school. Anna's teacher had agreed that Anna could go to the bathroom whenever her watch went off, even if she was in the middle of a lesson.

Anna practiced blowing up balloons while sitting on the toilet to increase her awareness of the muscles involved in pushing out stool, and practiced stopping and starting her urine stream to develop awareness and control over the feeling of urination. To help Anna strengthen the connection between her mind and body, she kept a journal where she recorded the feelings in her body before and after each meal. Slowly she learned to identify feelings of hunger and satiety. Sometimes she also noticed her bowels begin to stir after eating, and would go sit on the toilet.

When her efforts met with success, there was rejoicing in the house, and Anna was rewarded with a new Squinkie for her collection. Accidents were ignored, but Anna was taught to clean up after herself, and could do her own laundry by the time she was six.

Anna's parents enrolled her in a Tae Kwon Do class to help her develop mastery over her body and increase her self-esteem. Anna and her mother also engaged in sensory activities together, such as making bread, fingerpainting, walking barefoot in wet grass, and letting chocolate chips dissolve on their tongues. Shelly believed these experiences might help Anna be more aware of her senses; but, more important, they both enjoyed the time together. As their relationship improved, Anna began to confide in Shelly about her sadness and shame over her toileting problems. Shelly told Anna that she was also sad and ashamed that she had not understood what Anna was going through, and had been angry and harsh with her. Working as a team, the family was able to do the difficult work of helping Anna construct a mind-body connection that was missing from infancy.

CHAPTER 13

THE SCOOP ON POOP

By now I'm certain you've heard more about pooping than you ever wanted to know. Who knew it was so complicated! I hope you've recognized aspects of your situation with your child in the vignettes I've shared; and found some helpful information in this book. The good news is that encopresis is very responsive to treatment, especially if you address the three domains which both affect and are affected by the disorder - physical, behavioral, and emotional - in a coordinated approach. With your support, your child will ultimately learn to toilet herself independently. I'm not going to say you will look back on these days and laugh, because you probably won't; but you will look back and marvel at how far you and your child have come.

Speaking of which, let's see what's happened to Linda and Sam, who opened this book. Linda was desperate for information to help Sam, so she searched online and found a treatment protocol which recommended regular clean-outs with strong doses of laxatives and enemas. After two weeks of explosive diarrhea and holding down a screaming, thrashing child to administer enemas, Linda gave up. She resigned herself to living with Sam's soiling until a fateful (and rare) playdate. Linda was having coffee with Ryan's mother, Kate, when Sam had a huge accident, overflowed his pull-up, and got poop on Kate's kitchen floor. Linda thought she would die on the spot, but Kate responded by telling Linda that her older son had suffered with the same condition. Kate recommended the pediatric gastroenterologist she had consulted with her son, and Linda made an appointment immediately. The doctor was patient and kind with both Linda and Sam, as she explained encopresis and prescribed a medical regimen for Sam. The doctor recognized that Sam was fearful of making poop in the potty, and his fear was making his constipation and soiling worse; so she gave Linda the name of a therapist to work with them. Sam met with the therapist for weekly play therapy for nearly a year, while Linda and her husband, Jack, had monthly meetings with the therapist to develop strategies to use at home to help Sam. The therapist also worked with Sam's preschool, and the director allowed Sam to stay there as long as he was getting help.

Once Sam's constipation cleared up, the soiling stopped. Sam still refused to use the potty, but at least Linda was not changing poopy pull-ups several times a day! Eventually, Sam confessed to his therapist that he was very worried about the hole in his body and what might come out of him. Sam and the therapist worked on conquering that fear with a combination of education about how his body worked, and play aimed at mastering his anxiety about vulnerability and injury. Because Sam loved to draw, he and the therapist wrote and illustrated a book together called "The Adventures of Super Poopy Boy!" In a perfect example of life imitating art, just as "Super Poopy Boy" was winning the battle against the "Poop Monster," Sam won his own battle and made his first poop in the potty. Don't you love happy endings?

CONCLUSION

With the appropriate assessment and treatment, there will be a happy ending for you and your child too. I hope this book will play a part in your happy ending by helping you understand your child and his or her struggle with encopresis. We have explored several reasons children have difficulty mastering toileting: anxiety, hypersensitivity to internal and external sensations, hyposensitivity to internal and external sensations, inattention, and poor muscle tone and/or coordination of muscular activity. Knowing which factor, or combination of factors, makes potty training a challenge for your child is the first step towards a successful treatment plan.

Assembling a team to work with you and your child to address the physical, behavioral, and emotional obstacles blocking the path to the potty is a critical next step. With your team on the field, you can implement the strategies that will help your child win this fight. In the potty wars, victory can only be achieved when you and your child are allies in the battle against encopresis. Together, you can get out there and kick some poopy butt!

REFERENCES

American Academy of Pediatrics (n.d.) Parenting Corner Q&A: Soiling (Encopresis). Retrieved August 28, from http://www.aap.org/publiced/ BK5 Soiling.htm.

Boon, F.F.L. & Singh, N.N. (1991). A model for the treatment of encopresis. *Behavior Modification,* 15(3): 355-371.

Kuhn, B.R., Marcus, B.A., & Pitner, S.L. (1999). Treatment guidelines for primary nonretentive encopresis and stool toileting refusal. *American Family Physician,* 59(8):2171-2178.

McGrath, M.L., Mellon, M.W., & Murphy, L. (2000). Empirically supported treatments in pediatric psychology: constipation and encopresis. *Journal of Pediatric Psychology,* 25(4): 225-254.